HOUSES
FOR GOOD LIVING

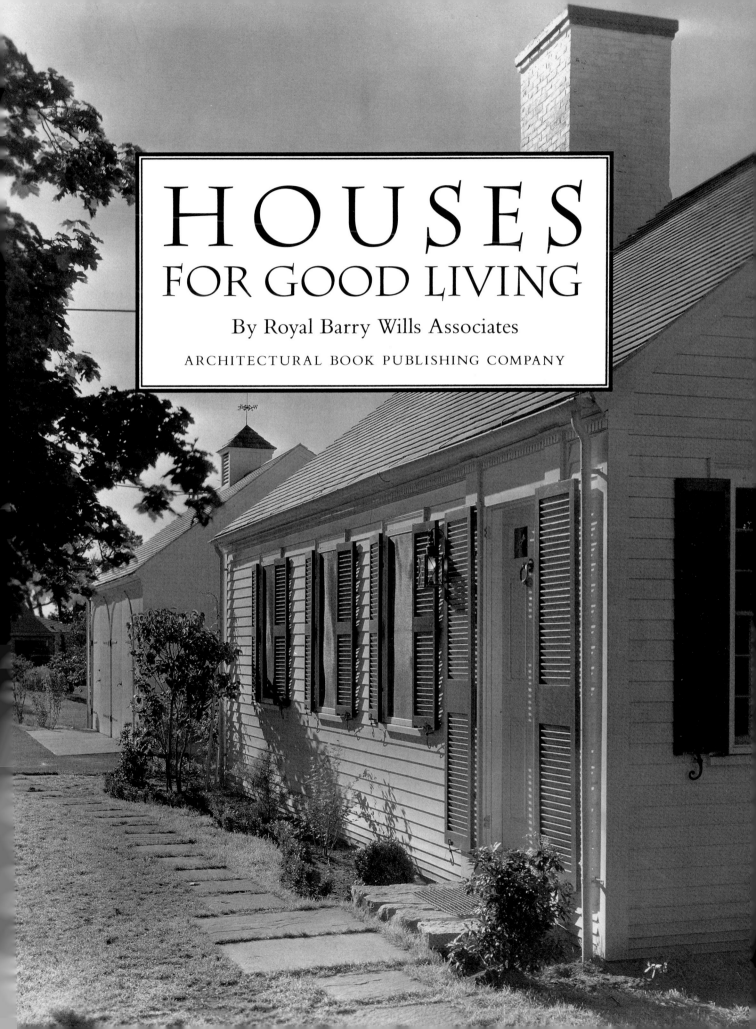

HOUSES
FOR GOOD LIVING

By Royal Barry Wills Associates

ARCHITECTURAL BOOK PUBLISHING COMPANY

ACKNOWLEDGMENTS

Royal Barry Wills Associates—Richard Wills, Jessica Barry Wills, Douglas Lipscomb and Robert Pesiri—wish to express their appreciation to all who expended their knowledge and efforts in the interest of the clients and the firm.

In particular:

Merton S. Barrows and Robert E. Minot, former associates whose delicate hands are reflected in some of the houses pictured.

Architectural photography is an art requiring the skill and ability of the artist and the patience of Job. To Alex Beatty, Fran Brennan, Mark Coté, Kenneth Duprey, Douglas Gilbert, Arthur Griffin, James Hooper, Vincent Lisanti, F. Dike Mason, Robert Mitchell, Fred Rola, Brian Vanden Brink, our thanks for picturing our work so well.

House and shelter publications are the architect's vehicle to show his work to the public. Thank you to *American Home, Better Homes and Gardens, Country Living, House Beautiful, House and Home* and *Houston Home and Garden* for their cooperation and permission to print previously published work.

AUTHOR'S NOTE

Some readers will find this volume contains houses published previously in Wills books. Because they are "classics" and as livable today as they were thirty or more years ago we choose to include them along with our more recent work.

Library of Congress Cataloging-in-Publication Data

Houses for good living / Royal Barry Wills Associates.
      p.   cm.
      Rev. ed. of: More houses for good living.
      ISBN 0-942655-07-9
      1. Architecture, Domestic.   2. Architecture,
Domestic—Designs and plans.   I. Royal Barry Wills
Associates.   II. Title: More houses for good living.
NA7120.H86   1993
728′.37—dc20   93-17789
                                                                    CIP

FOREWORD

It could almost be called a cult—so great remains the affection in the housing industry for the late Royal Barry Wills.

Few, if any, architects ever commanded such a following.

His name is still alive, practically the symbol of the ultimate objective in the hopes of countless couples planning or buying a house.

This tribute, of course, belongs in no small measure to his associates, who are not merely carrying on a famous name but who are adding their individual design talents to the task of improving our environment.

Richard Wills interned under a great master. His father taught him the familiar trademarks of early American houses, lines that have endured for generations because of their classic beauty. But he and the younger associates have developed individual skills, and if, on the following pages, you find the familiar fat chimney, the low eave and the cheerful small-pane windows, you will also find these happy details complemented by new materials, new uses of glass, designs that extend comfortable interiors to delightful terraces and views—and new uses that make a Wills house as functional today as the first salt-box of our settlers.

WILLIAM E. DORMAN
Boston Herald Traveler
Real Estate Editor

CONTENTS

Royal Barry Wills in front of his own home.

ROYAL BARRY WILLS AND THE HISTORY OF THE FIRM

From its seventeenth-century beginnings the crafting of the New England house achieved a timeless excellence, a felicitous composition of simple details in the snug, domestic scale that still charms us. Through the years, as pioneering was succeeded by a measure of security and affluence, the house evolved handsome and more ornate variations, until its mid-nineteenth-century confrontation with a fast developing industrial land that had lost touch with beauty. Later, after century's turn, a few architects along the eastern seaboard began to resurrect the prototype, or reasonable facsimile thereof, but almost none was discerning enough to avoid clumsiness in design, or quite able to shed the influence of architectural aberrations he had, inevitably, been bred to. The average small house was still conceived and executed in high-posted ugliness, replete with a few wood turnings and a little jig-sawn scroll-work to give it class. Yet the physical re-creation and the enduring virtues of our early houses were to be restored to us and, by common agreement among many fellow professionals, the man who achieved the miracle was Royal Barry Wills.

Of course it behooves a New Englander never to forget that the world is full of areas with valid images, and who's to proclaim the most worthy among them, and in reference to what scale of values? Yet where could one ever behold a more *simpatico* melding of intimate landscape and simple, attractive houses than hereabouts—at least where industry hasn't cast its blight? The ancestral plowshares may have turned up a few stones and the climate may have had its harsh moments, but what an Eden of small green valleys, ponds and little streams, in which to build their trim, white domiciles, fronted in time by towering elms or maples! Here was a social continuity where families bred and succeeded one another, adding wings, or barns as the need arose. Our assessment and use of this heritage is based on an appreciation of its physical charms and their adaptability to our present needs but, too, there is an inevitable residue of affection for the homes that sheltered our sturdy ancestors in the days before trailer living, fly-now-and-pay-later and the credit card.

For years the average small house had been of uncertain lineage, the product of vestigial talent out of a Victorian inheritance and, furthermore, of little pecuniary interest to the emerging profession of architecture. It could hardly have been otherwise at the time, because our major offices served the new wealth and smaller, less grandiose practitioners took the less profitable leavings. They had to make a living and eschewed house design because one could never turn a fair profit for his efforts. That was the accepted gospel except, perhaps, with the young Royal Barry Wills.

He had grown up in Melrose, a northerly suburb of Boston, and entered Massachusetts Institute of Technology with the class of 1918. Having chosen the stern discipline of architectural engineering with no record of early design predilections, he contributed many a hilarious cartoon to Institute publications throughout his four years as an undergraduate. They terminated at a troubled time in the world's affairs, when fate's common graduation present was professional frustration and an invitation to join the armed services. Wills accepted his without historical comment and chose the Navy. Thereafter a still laggard postwar building industry prompted him to sign with William Cramp and Sons shipyard, until Boston's Turner Construction Company provided a berth in its design department.

The experience was a happy one but somewhere along the tortuous way, from his freshman year at M.I.T., Royal Barry Wills had come to realize that the New England house was his forte and consuming interest, not in its then contemporary ugliness, but in versions of the clean, simple prototype his forebears had built in earlier Massachusetts days.

Fortuitously he had a vision because, in retrospect, the probability of failure was discouragingly high. His natural shyness quite denied him the brash plausibility of a salesman and there was no wealth to backlog the adventure, no useful social prestige to help launch it. The degree of his design talent was not then apparent, because it had not been unleashed, but two basic assets were there for his friends to observe. He could police his visions with Yankee common sense and push them to a trial, even against the inertia of a protesting shyness. True, the entree to architectural practice was less difficult through house design than many another route but always there loomed the formidable problem of attracting clients. Wills' reticence worked to make him a complete conformist to the prohibitions against direct selling but luckily it was not acute enough to preclude the indirect approach.

He hit upon a device that might work when a Boston newspaper agreed to publish his sections and sketches that would be of interest both to advertisers and readers, displaying the wares of one for the delectation of the other. In return the paper would direct inquiries for architectural advice to him. And it succeeded, by easy stages, while he worked days for Turner and devoted his evenings to the grand plan. Came the moment when a woman responded to his lure and an appointment was arranged. Wills withdrew from active circulation for several hours to cudgel himself into the state of reckless courage necessary for meeting Client Number One.

What transpired on that epochal occasion is unrecorded and of importance only as it came to mark the first of many such. The trickle of voluntary clients continued and, as it does not take many to keep a sole-proprietor busy full time, he opened a one-room office on lower Beacon Street in 1925. **Royal Barry Wills, Architect** was lettered on the door, to announce the start of a practice that has been continuous, even through the depression and World War II.

The Wills philosophy of architecture, as it pertained to the small house, was the basic reason for his success. Spread through New England were examples of every stylistic adventure the house had since 1680 and the ones of enduring excellence were the simple, indigenous Colonial variations on one- and two-story themes, whose similitude was easy and economical to achieve, using stock materials. Others had made that general observation but almost nobody had caught the subtle interrelationship of elements and the restraints that gave a scale and charm, really to bring it off.

The Cape Cod Cottage, so-called, was his natural choice for a minimal house, but one whose simplicity had minute controls. It was always low to the ground, with eaves just above its windows. There would be an outsized central chimney and a roof pitch that ranged from 8 inches to 10 inches, vertically, in 12 inches of run. The sash were made up of from twenty-four to thirty-six individual lights, and clapboards were graduated from a 2³/₄-inch exposure at the foundation to a typical 4-inch that was continued from top of window sill to eave. Thus to mention a few tenets of design that contributed to its palpable charm.

From lower Beacon Street the Wills office moved to Beacon Hill for a long stay—the period of its climb to pre-eminence. Always small in personnel concerned, its successful operation was predicated on the ability of a few experts, who did not need a dictionary to supply their architectural and construction vocabularies. Initially there was Perry Tufts and, later, Merton S. Barrows and Robert E. Minot. In the beginning Wills set up the sketch plans for each commission and, after approval, followed them with a large freehand perspective that he made with astonishing ease and speed. It was sent to the client and prints of it served as guides in the evolution of working drawings.

In the good old unregenerate days, before gadgetry and the complications of "modern living" raised their fevered heads, the inward house of our ancestors (with such modest additions as electric lights, central heat and plumbing) served as well as its classic exterior, and that obtained through the Twenties. Responsive to public trends, Royal Barry Wills had no qualms about the adaptability of his design system to changing mores. In its slow growth the New England house had developed from a one-room cottage upward and outward, adding wings, ells, sheds, barns and leantos in picturesque profusion, yet always within the demands of that priceless sense of scale that set it apart from the ruck of later housework. The technicality of "scale" defies easy definition and is quite the most difficult thing to describe. It involves the relation of parts comprising a whole, their size and shape, their seeming felicity, one to another, and inevitably one's assessment stems from long experience. Whatever the Philistine reaction, scale has utter validity and its quality is recognized by anyone who cares deeply for a form of design in the traditional manner, or even in the eclectic variations that Wills managed so successfully in the Thirties. They were less a change in body than in clothing, always using natural materials but with board and batten and brick or stone.

Throughout that period he won eight or more competitive awards in national contests, had a feature article in *Life* magazine and later, in the *Saturday Evening Post*. The professional publications and others were constantly running illustrated pieces about him and his work. There was a Certificate of Honor from the Massachusetts State Association of Architects in 1949 and the ultimate accolade, a fellowship in the American Institute of Architects, in 1954. Yet all the while he ran a small office, based on the indisputable fact that the profit margin is slender in house design and quite vanishes except in an organization of a very few, skillful men. Robert E. Minot and Merton S. Barrows had joined him in the mid-Thirties, after schooling at M.I.T. and with New England architectural forms much a part of their background. They became his chief assistants, as building revived after the depression, and carried a prime responsibility in an expanding practice that pretty much covered this country, along with excursions into Canada and the tropics. Inevitably the New England idiom had its area limitations, or a client had her heart set on French Provincial, so the firm produced delightful houses of different genres and in the contemporary manner. The Wills office ventured slightly from its chosen field in 1941, when it designed a 300-unit housing complex for defense workers at Springfield, Lucy Mallory Village, for which it received federal commendations.

During World War II Mr. Wills held the quiet professional fort with his secretary while his young men were soldiering, and the then unexacting task of being one's own draftsman was not too onerous to prevent a return to watercolors, at which he had a true flair. Wills, somehow, had come by the priceless gift of being able to concern himself with microscopic detail where it counted or slough off any concern for it when he was wielding a sable brush loaded with Windsor and Newton's pigment. As the office re-formed for the busy post-war years it was very much of a "going concern," permitting its founder more time for his hobbies, which included, besides authoring, a very fair skill at tennis and ancient compulsion to attend auctions.

Warren J. Rhoter joined the office in 1948 and Richard Wills in 1952, both assuming managerial status when the firm became Royal Barry Wills and Associates in 1957. At the time of Mr. Wills' death, in 1962, and activation of a corporation, his principal associates were able to carry on because of the foresighted arrangement.

Inevitably the firm has broadened its field and, if not purposefully, at least with the same skilled touch that characterizes its domestic work. Of course the houses, at quarter scale, have long since grown beyond the limits of a double-elephant drawing board, and there have been handsome churches, along with the large operation of Rossmoor Leisure World in New Jersey, a corporate Headquarters in Hampton, New Hampshire and cluster housing projects throughout New England. But Royal Barry Wills Associates will always be a relatively small, skilled organization and no place for a congenital basker with limited application. It has been accorded many a professional honor since 1925, and those of us who have known the office for over forty years still marvel at Royal's initial vision, at his disciplined purpose and unending restraint. He wanted only to design the indigenous New England house supremely well and succeeded beyond any other architect. It was a most happy circumstance that the public and his fellow architects honored him so signally in his own time.

Richard Wills, who studied architecture at The Boston Architectural Center with the added privilege of tutelage from his famous father, leads the firm today. The third generation family member, Jessica Barry Wills, joined the firm in 1986. She and her father, Richard, are ably assisted by associates Douglas Lipscomb and Robert Pesiri in Boston and Lynn Talacko at the Newcastle, Maine office.

THE DEVELOPMENT OF
THE COLONIAL HOUSE

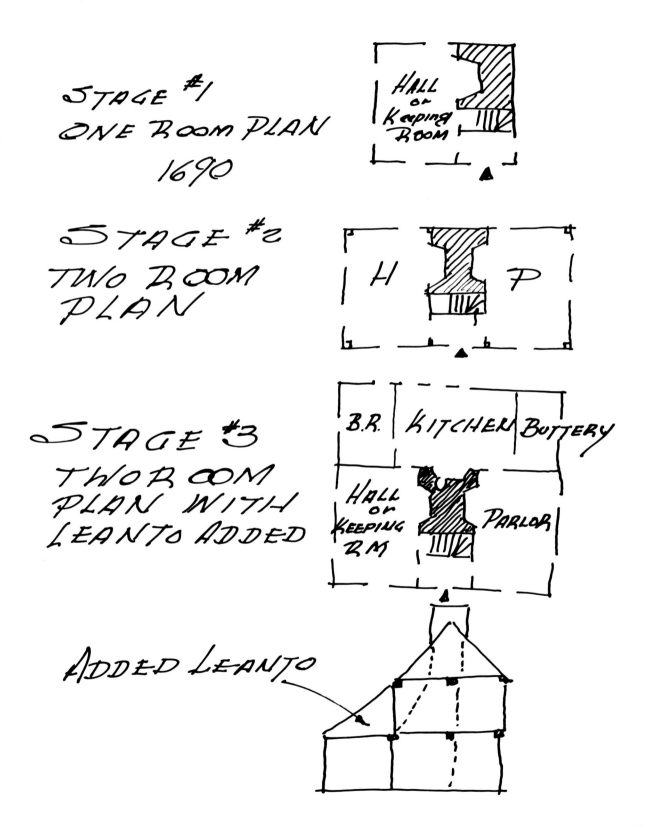

STAGE #1
ONE ROOM PLAN
1690

HALL or Keeping Room

STAGE #2
TWO ROOM PLAN

H   P

STAGE #3
TWO ROOM PLAN WITH LEANTO ADDED

B.R. | KITCHEN | BUTTERY

HALL or KEEPING RM   PARLOR

ADDED LEANTO

GOOD CAPE COD HOUSES ARE LIKE THIS

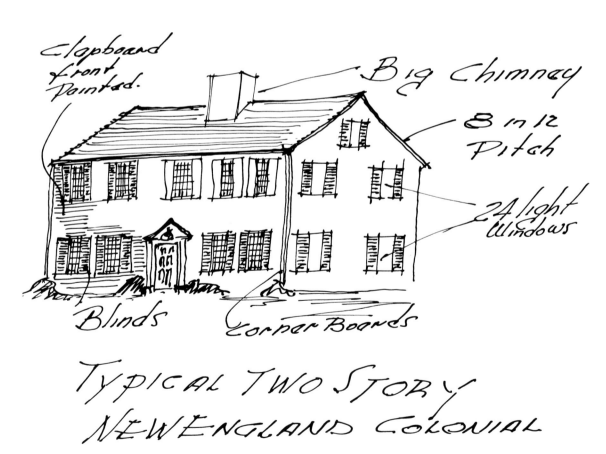

Roof pitch Not too Steep 8/12 is typical

Nice big chimney

Close Cornice

Set close to ground

Raised Panel door

Low Story height 7'-0" to 7'-6"

Clapboards 4" to Weather

12 light or 24 light Windows - close under eaves

Clapboard front Painted.

Big Chimney

8 in 12 Pitch

24 light Windows

Blinds

Corner Boards

TYPICAL TWO STORY NEW ENGLAND COLONIAL

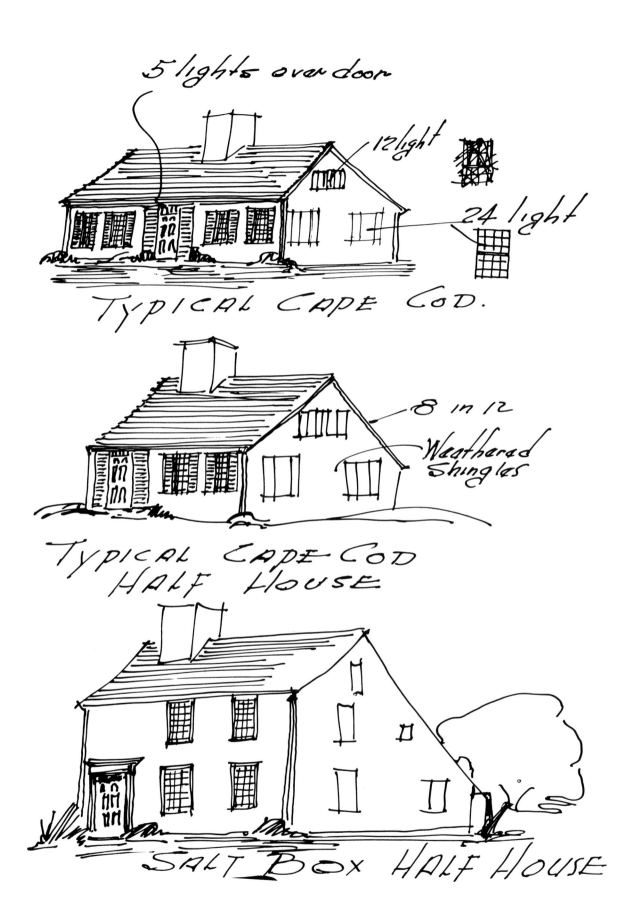

5 lights over door

12 light

24 light

TYPICAL CAPE COD.

8 in 12

Weathered Shingles

TYPICAL CAPE COD HALF HOUSE

SALT BOX HALF HOUSE

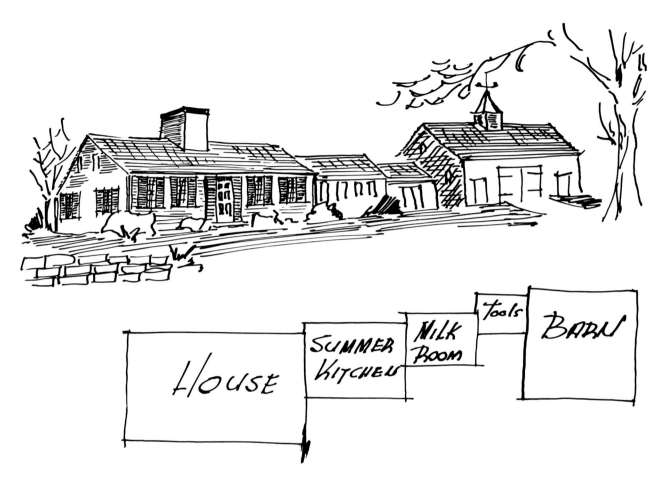

House | Summer Kitchen | Milk Room | Tools | BARN

Colonial Houses had many dependancies
At least the farmhouse did.

Cape Cod houses were often Sea Captains
houses & so did not have as many sheds
as say New Hampshire Houses.

TYPICAL SALT BOX
WITH CENTER ENTRANCE

Steeper roof
Stained Clapboards

TYPICAL GARRISON

HIP ROOF HOUSE

More Elaborate
Entrance

Elaborate CORNICE

TYPICAL NANTUCKET HOUSE

Windows tall & Narrow
Weathered Shingles
Widows Walk
Picket Fence right up to front door
House set close to street

BUCK'S COUNTY, PA.

Pennsylvania Dutch Houses
Were mostly Of stone
Note raised panel shutters &
Wide Cornice Board.

COMMON MISTAKES
IN
"COLONIAL" HOUSES
as built today

Too steep roof

Too low roof is bad too

Clumsy Dormers

Too High Story

Too Wide overhang

Chimney skimpy & awkward location

Mullion Windows not in keeping

Trick Shutters in bad taste

Horizontal panes— bad

House too high off ground too many steps

Picture Windows out of Scale

Windows often too fat & short or bad shape panes

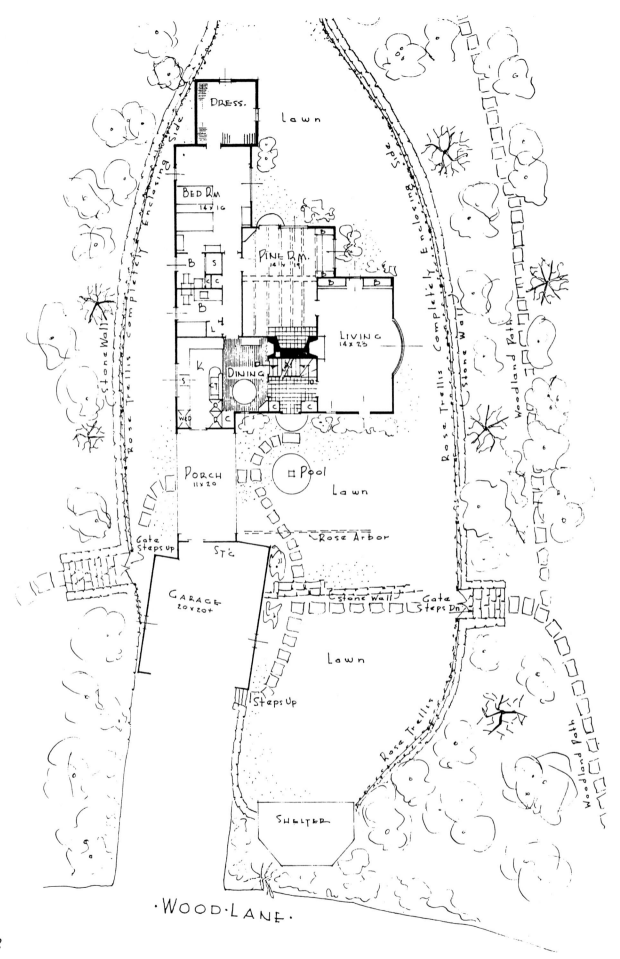

DRESS.

lawn

BED RM
14 x 16

B   S
C C
B

PINE RM.
14 x 19

LIVING
14 x 23

K
S
CT
O
WRD   C

DINING

PORCH
11 x 20

□ Pool

Lawn

Rose Arbor

Gate
Steps up

ST'G

GARAGE
20 x 20+

Stone Wall

Gate
Steps Dn

Lawn

Steps Up

SHELTER

Stone Wall   Rose Trellis   completely   Enclosing Side

Rose Trellis   Completely   Enclosing Side   Stone Wall

Woodland Path

Rose Trellis

Woodland Path

· WOOD · LANE ·

Royal Barry Wills' own house is set in an oval wall rose garden, which was once part of an old estate not far from Boston. Old handsplit cypress shingles were used for the gambrel roof, and antique clapboards cover the walls. The massive corbeled chimney is a Wills hallmark.

x

x

Winchester, Mass. 23

The tiny stair hall is reminiscent of the hall in the Capen House in Topsfield, built in the seventeenth century. It shows Mr. Wills' careful concern for authentic detail.

A minute fireplace is tucked into a corner of the dining area. Delightful in its simplicity.

The study in Mr. Wills' house has all the elements of the atmosphere of which he personally enjoyed. A large fireplace made of old bricks with old oak lintel, old beams, pine sheathing and rough plaster.

The wing and ells reflect the plan. Varied materials of whitewashed brick, clapboards and vertical siding add texture and interest. The main focus and orientation is toward the historic copper beech silhouetted in the background.

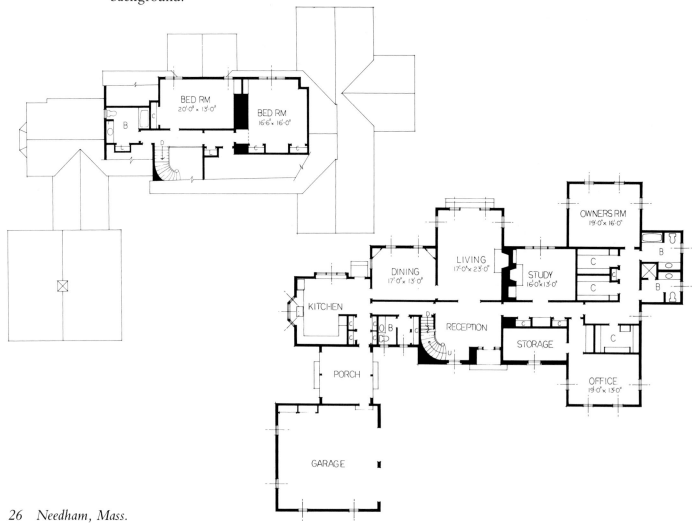

A true interpretation of the Spirit of New England. The house strings out
with various appendages to the rear.

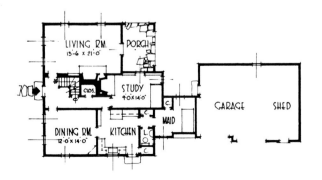

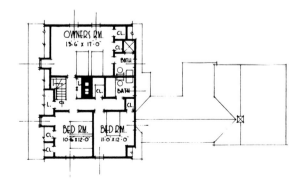

Simple in detail, yet majestic, as the shadows play on the whitewashed brick facade and hand-split shake roof.

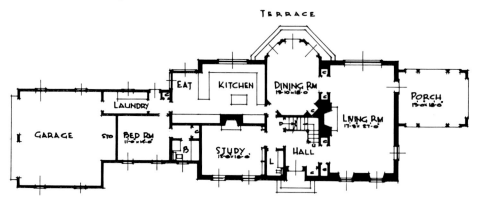

The warmth of stained wood and the detail of the paneling and mantel bid welcome for a few hours of leisure in the study.

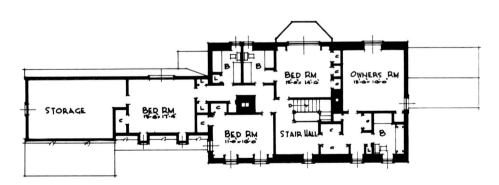

This was one of Royal Barry Wills' last houses, and while most of the homes shown in this book are the result of cooperative effort the entrance porch pictured here shows Mr. Wills' personal touch.

The site is beautifully landscaped and features an extensive collection of azaleas.

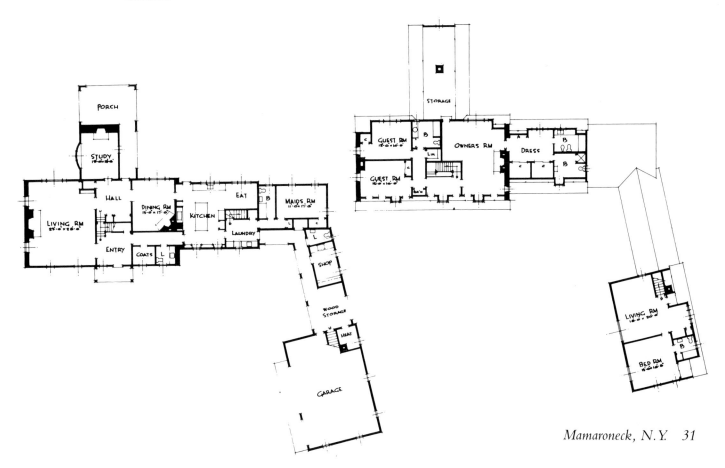

A spacious entrance hall is paved with old square bricks. The closed stringer stair with turned balusters gives access to bedrooms on the second floor.

The dining room
furnished with fine
antiques has a pilastered
fireplace breast. A
horizontal sheathed dado
is used on the other
walls.

The study is lighted by a
many-paned bow
window. Old beam and
board ceiling and floor
provide a background for
appropriate furnishings.

The courtyard of cobblestone laid in a circular pattern is the *piece de resistance*.

Built in a suburb of Boston, this house has walls veneered with second-hand brick, which has been whitewashed.

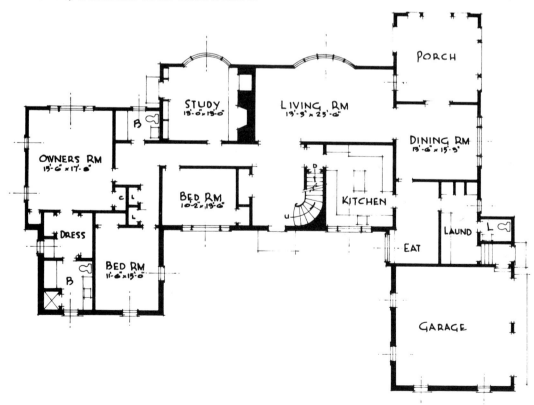

Halfway up a steep hillside in Peterborough, New Hampshire, this house has two large bow windows commanding a magnificent view. The fence is not just decorative. It serves a utilitarian purpose. The owner keeps horses that graze on the land; the fence protects the lawn.

If one climbs farther up the hill the entire house and the view can be seen in a glance. Also evident is how attractive the Colonial house is with its various wings and appendages.

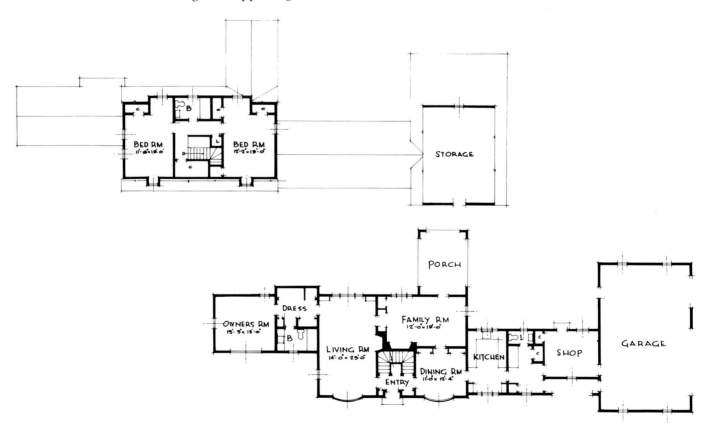

This fine example of the New England farm house form is surrounded by open fields. Narrow clapboards are painted barn-red; the trim is white. A large bow window dominates the living room.

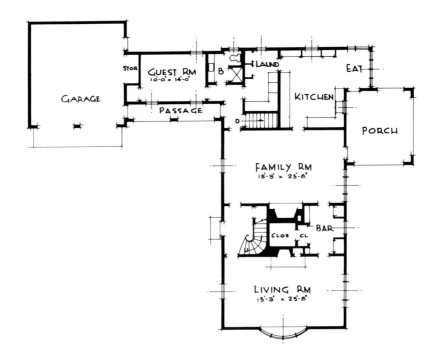

The large family dining room is the depth of the house. The shelves at one
end display a fine collection of pewter.

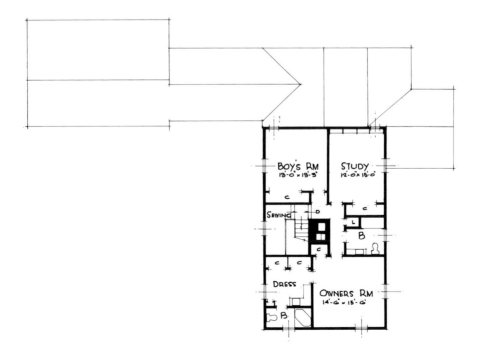

This home is built on a point of land just outside one of the loveliest towns in New England. Built practically at the edge of the water, a terrace at the rear overlooks a picturesque harbor.

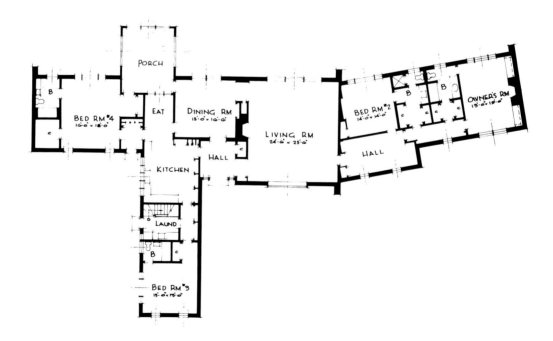

An enclosed porch has glass on three sides and a practical floor paved with bluestone. The deck beyond is set up with comfortable furniture for outdoor living.

The high studded walls, end chimneys and triple dormers add sophistication
to the story and one half design.

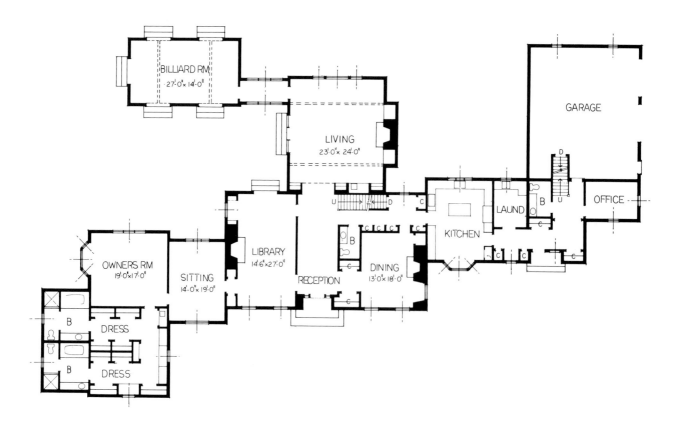

A close-up of the main façade. Note the pilastered, recessed entrance with sidelights and transom.

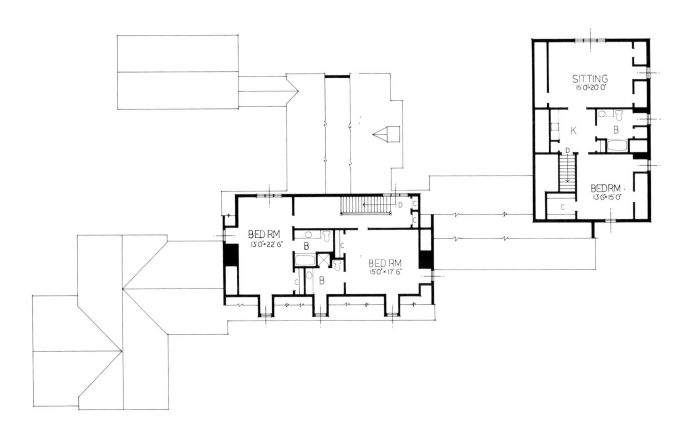

37 Apple Hill Lane was the product of a team of architects, a land-development firm and sixty independent builders working together to find ways to build the best possible houses. It is New England Colonial in its inspiration, but split concrete block was used for the walls. Long-wearing aluminum was used for the roof. A graceful pilastered front entrance with double doors is topped by a leaded-glass transom to give the façade a fine focal point.

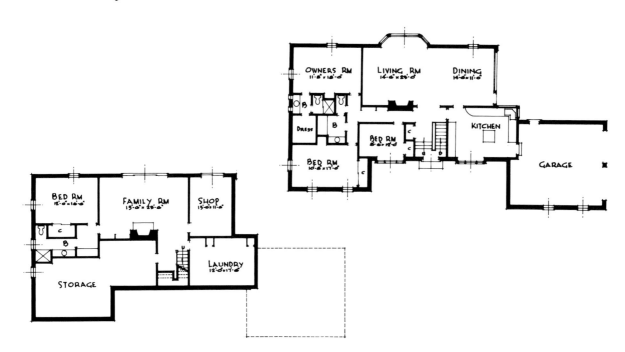

Outdoor living at its best! The giant checkers and checkerboard terrace serve a multi-purpose: entertainment while the picnic is cooking on the grille, then tables and stools for serving and eating.

Restoration is part of Royal Barry Wills Associates practice. This 1800 farm
house has been carefully restored with slight interior modifications for
contemporary living. The carriage barn was originally a one-room school
house moved to the site in 1876.

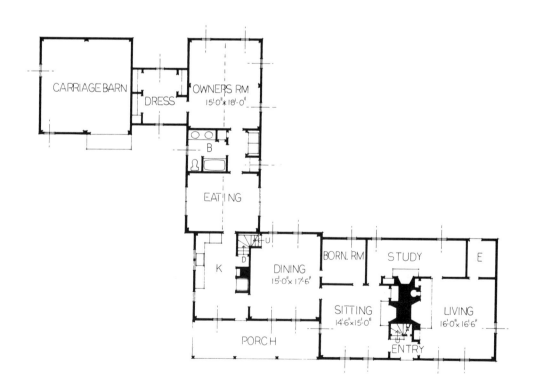

The sitting room, or "front parlor" if you will, has hand troweled plaster walls and wide board wainscot.

The living room. Hand planed wide pumpkin pine boards cover the walls.

Once the wood shed, now master bedroom, with the original post and beam frame and wood ceiling.

The breakfast room.

There are many types of gambrel roofs. This one is not as steep as those found in Connecticut, nor does it have the overhang at the eaves of the Dutch gambrel found on Long Island.

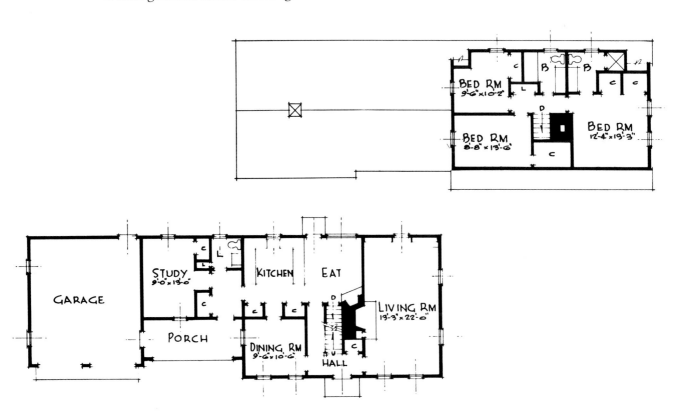

One of Royal Barry Wills' houses at Cohasset is this charmer, built on a ledge overlooking Massachusetts Bay. His hobby of attending auctions and prowling around used building material yards paid off here. The majority of exterior and interior material is reclaimed and recycled.

From the terrace on the ocean side one has an unlimited view of the water.

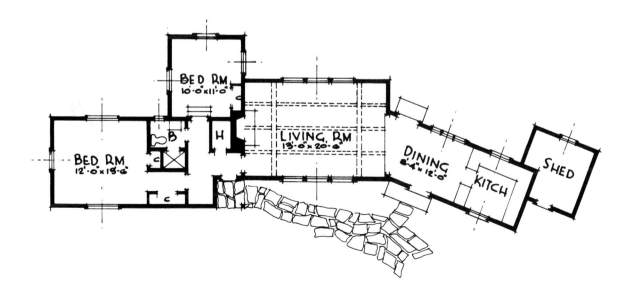

The fireplace wall is paneled with
old doors and shutters. At the left,
beyond the front entry, is a glimpse
of the bedroom.

At the end of the dining area two
scalloped cupboards provide space
for decorative as well as useful
objects. Behind the shutter doors is
a small but efficient kitchen.

Another gambrel-roofed home with two large bay windows that enhance rather than detract from the façade even though they would never be found in an old house of an earlier century.

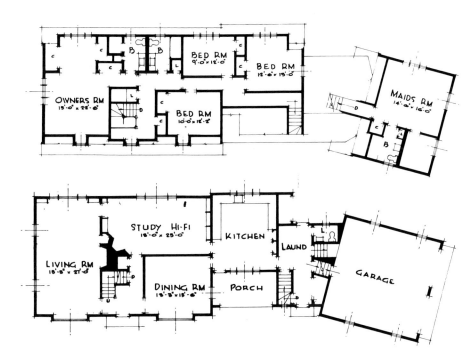

Overlooking Buzzards Bay on Cape Cod, this house is reminiscent of the larger old houses found in the area. The main section, however, is made of whitewashed brick instead of the conventional white-cedar shingles or clapboards, giving it a more formal aspect.

The study is paneled in walnut.

Separating the kitchen and a formal dining room is a breakfast area. From the large window one can see the water of Buzzards Bay.

The prototype of this house is the early eighteenth-century farmhouse. The roof at the back swoops down to the top of the first-floor windows, forming a design of the salt-box type. Stained clapboards have been used with white painted trim. Note the detailed brickwork on the chimney.

The spacious keeping room at the back of the house has a large window and door to a terrace. Its large fireplace has an old beam lintel with a curved plaster wall over it. The atmosphere is one of the early eighteenth century.

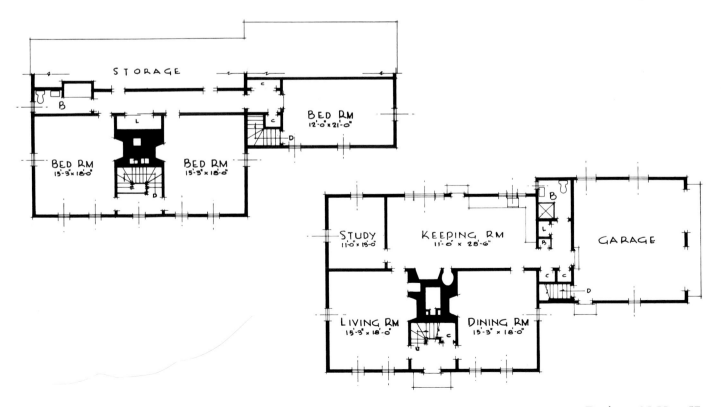

The idea of Emil Hanslin, land planner and developer, Bright Coves is the first of a series of vacation retirement villages lying between Hyannis and Falmouth, in Mashpee. The area on Nantucket Sound, the warm-water side of Cape Cod, is called New Seabury. This is one of the houses designed for the complex. It retains the general elements of the Cape Cod cottage, such as the roof lines and oversized chimney, but the details are contemporary. The combination is refreshing.

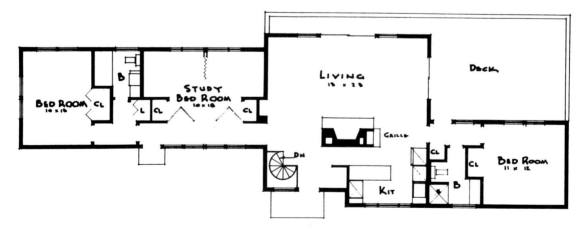

The living room and master bedroom are extended to the sun deck by sliding glass doors. The upper deck and lower level are devoted to indoor-outdoor multi-use.

From the deck, the main living area in the summer, can be seen the sparkling waterways of Bright Coves.

During the colder months a friendly fireplace serves as the center of attraction. Contemporary in design, it retains the old beam lintel and a herringbone rectangle of an earlier day as decoration.

A house with unusual eye appeal. Clapboard siding and weathered shingles on the main section and vertical sheathing on the wing is an interesting combination of materials that complements the delightful state-of-Maine countryside setting. The roof is a half-gambrel—not as prevalent as the full gambrel or straight gable found on most old New England cottages.

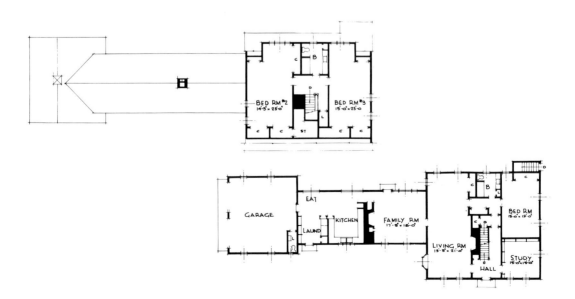

A Regency-style house built in a suburb of Boston. This type of house is not usually associated with the Wills office, but it illustrates the fact that good design training is not limited to one period of architecture.

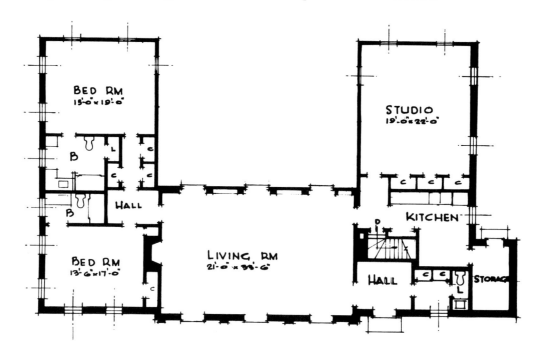

The living room occupies the whole of the center section of the plan. Three double doors open to a formal garden designed by the owner.

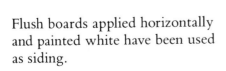

Flush boards applied horizontally and painted white have been used as siding.

The living room was designed and detailed to complement the client's antique furniture.

This house was designed for clients who preferred an old house but did not want to take on the upkeep of one. Whitewashed brick has been used for the facade. The ends are white-cedar shingles left to weather. Flush boards have been used on the kitchen wing at the right.

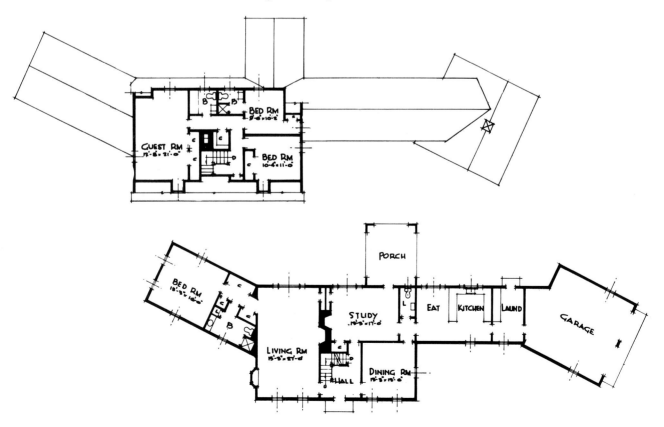

Colonial houses had many appendages. This one, built in Brookline,
Massachusetts, shows how the idea can be successfully adapted to a house
for modern living. While the garage is in front, it is unobtrusive.

Inside the entrance court
a simple entrance has a
pair of doors and an
arched transom.

The random articulated brickwork adds texture and shadow to the facade, restraining the formality of the design.

Although in a resort area this house is used all year round. The main house at the right was existing; a new wing containing a new entrance hall, large living room and master bedroom suite was added.

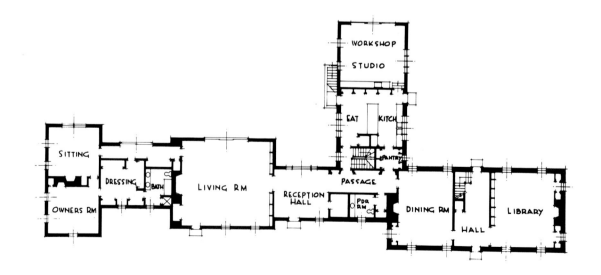

The new wing viewed from the porch of the existing house.

Used brick, weathered barn boards and hand split cedar shingles are an interesting combination of color and texture that blends well with the rocky coastal setting.

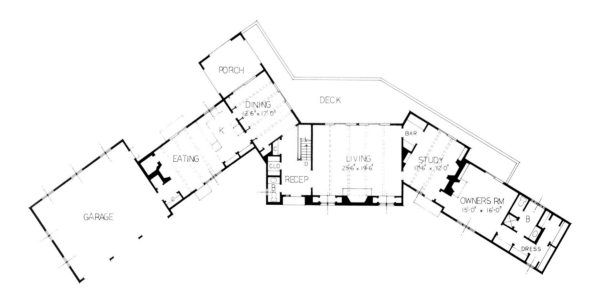

"A room with a view", to coin a phrase.

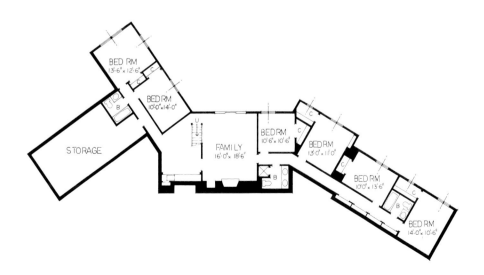

Above and opposite:
A good example of using the elements of traditional design in an original fashion. The result is refreshing and pleasing to the eye without being stereotyped.

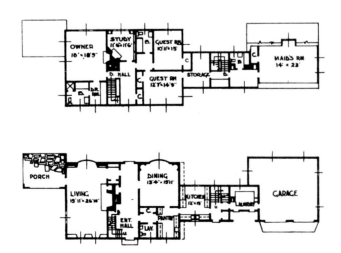

Large bow windows were not found in the early houses of the American colonies. However, had the inhabitants had our efficient heating systems, a bow window such as this one probably would have been used. The set of Chippendale chairs in combination with good architectural details makes this dining room a handsome one.

A spacious entrance hall runs the depth of the house. The wide front door
with rim lock is paneled.

A Dutch door is used
for the rear entrance.

The rolling open field dictated the multi-level plan. The main section is used brick, whitewashed, lending a touch of informality to the façade.

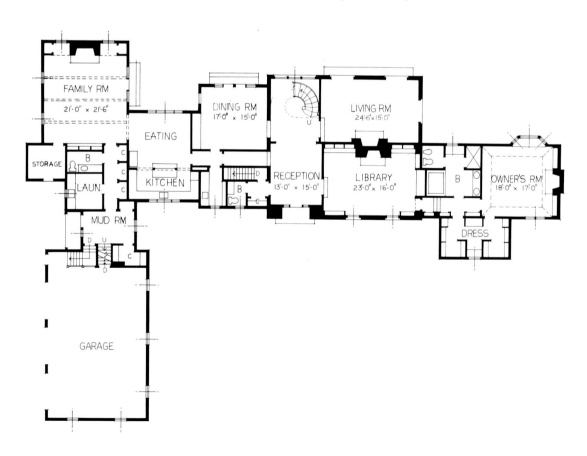

The two story window at the end of the main entrance hall is background for the gracefully curving stair.

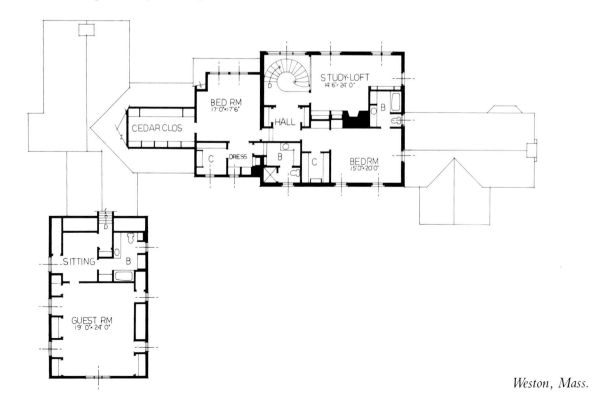

The main stair with two story window behind and "Wills" to greet you.

The family room with the fieldstone chimney and wood beam trusses lends
an air of informality conducive to relaxation. Television and audio
equipment are built into the cabinet on the left.

Built in a very old town north of Boston, this gambrel-roofed house takes on the character of its environment. Diamond-paned windows have been used with stained narrow clapboards. The imposing tall chimney anchors the house firmly to its wooded site.

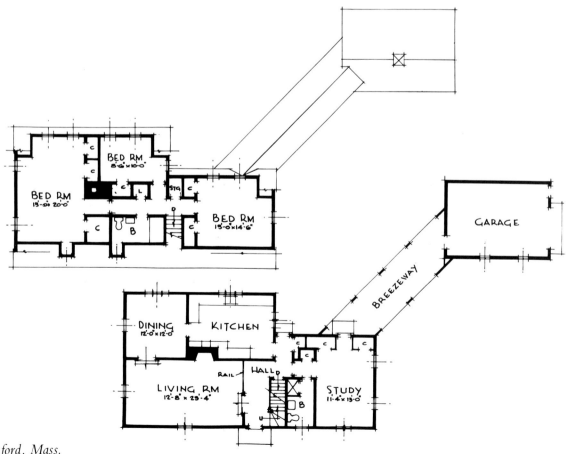

Not all new houses are as fortunate as this one, with its fine antique furnishings. Notable are the highboy with cabriole legs and ball-and-claw feet and the corner chair with pierced splats.

The fireplace wall is sheathed with old wide pine boards while directly over the fireplace panels have been used to relieve the severity.

Cooking over an open fire has an attraction for most chefs. The owner finds this arrangement most satisfactory.

Simple details as the corner drops at the overhang, "V" gutters and oversized corbeled chimney add interest to the "Garrison" style.

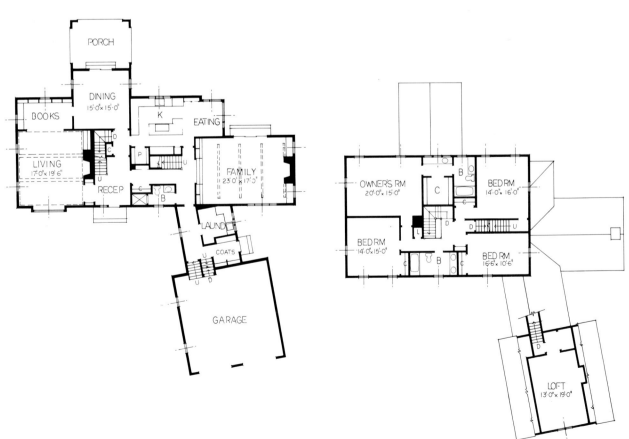

Sunlight and shadow on whitewashed brick entrance, a simple formal
façade. Heavy dormers would have been disastrous. These are an asset to
the total design.

This design is further enhanced by the use of the brick wall. Without it the house would still be attractive, but the wall's presence here serves to pull the various wings into one unit and form an entrance court.

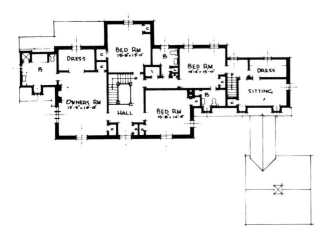

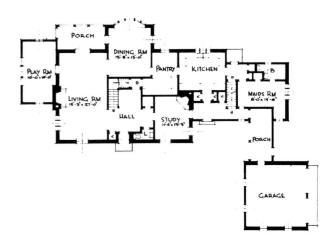

This "Cape" style design rambles as many of its ancestors, with wings and ells emanating from the central structure.

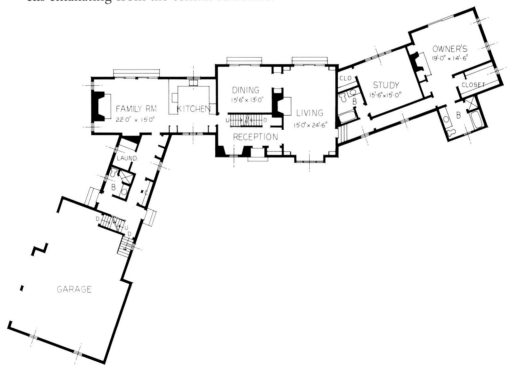

This house is less typical than others. To take advantage of a sloping site the house is two stories in the rear. It has a combination of materials—stone, flush boards and battens and rough-sawn clapboards.

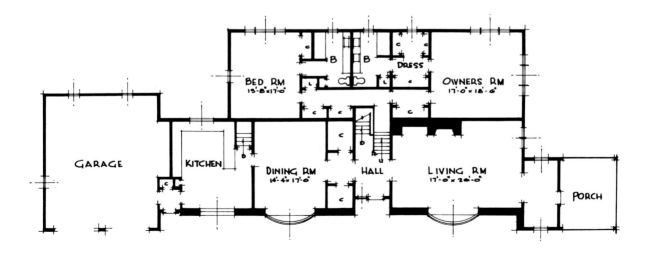

This restrained façade reminds one of the simple farmhouses found all over
New England. The understated entrance vestibule is made even more
pleasing by lilac shrubs on either side.

The stable, painted barn-red with white trim, as is the house, looks as if it
had been on the site for two centuries.

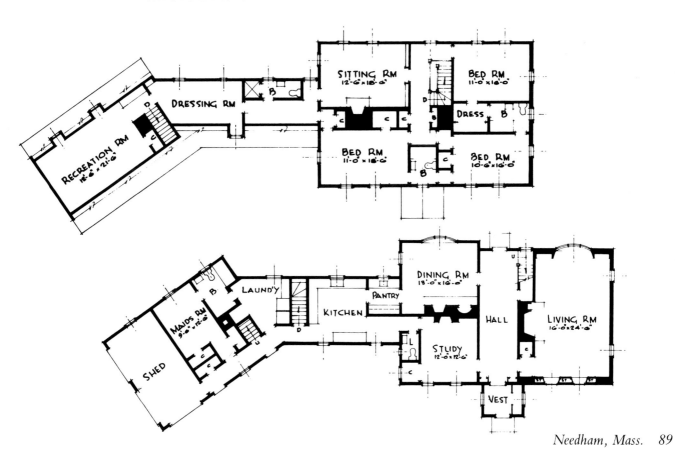

This house has all the elements of a Wills design. Low to the ground, with graduated clapboards at the foundation, cornice just above twelve over twelve small-paned windows, a pleasing roof pitch, all topped by a massive chimney.

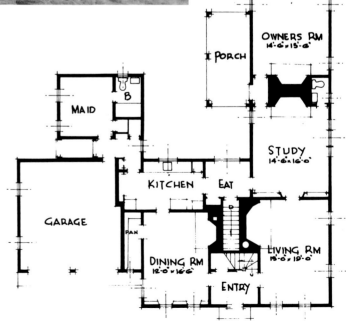

A room in the basement provides an attractive area for informal entertaining and parties. Many of the details are worth noting. The shelf with an off-center bracket is an example of fine attention to detail that raises a design above the commonplace.

Another example of an authentic seventeenth-century stair. While a stair of this type would not be found in an old Cape Cod cottage, its use here does not seem out of order. Paint has been used instead of natural wood and the floor has been spattered.

The Wills office likes to use old materials in restoration and reconstructions.
The main entrance to the remodeled 150 year old barn was reclaimed from a
nearby wrecking yard.

One half of the 20′ × 50′ barn has been made into an L-shaped living room, one section of which is used for dining. The walls are sheathed with wide pine boards and an old beam found on the beach runs across the ceiling.

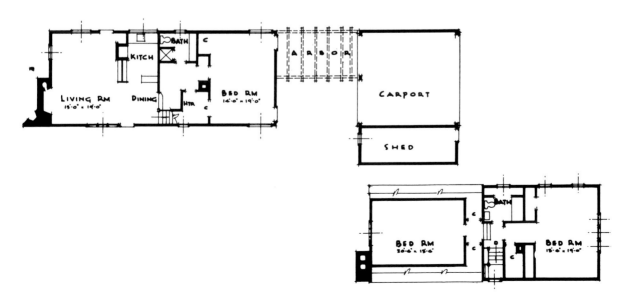

The treads and risers, giving access to two oversized bedrooms on the second floor, are made of solid blocks of wood cut from an old beam.

The area in which this house was built (Cape Ann) has a plentiful supply of stones. Ground cover has been used instead of grass for easy maintenance.

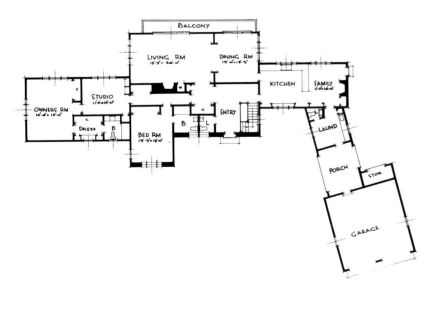

The beautifully landscaped house above is built on a difficult rocky site in Wellesley, Massachusetts. The main section is of whitewashed brick and on the service wing and garage wide flush boards have been used.

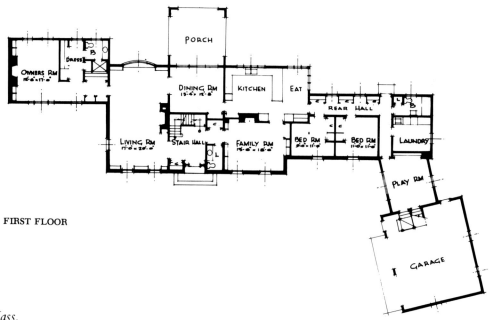

FIRST FLOOR

The study is paneled in walnut. Slate is used for the fireplace facing and the interior of the fireplace is soapstone instead of the conventional brick.

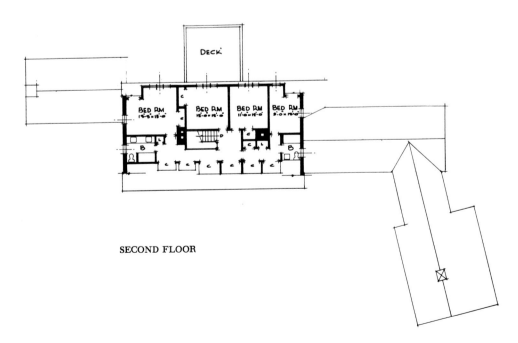

SECOND FLOOR

This addition to a house built in the Colonial style during the nineteen-thirties clearly illustrates how outdoor living can be achieved in a traditional home simply by opening the rear with sliding glass doors. The front (not shown) is quite conventionally traditional.

The narrow deck provides access from the living room to a spacious brick terrace.

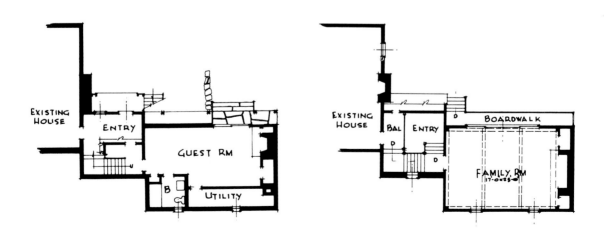

Typical of many of the early Eighteenth-century houses along the New England coast, this center entrance hip roof design sits snugly on the crest of a slope with a view of Pemaquid Harbor.

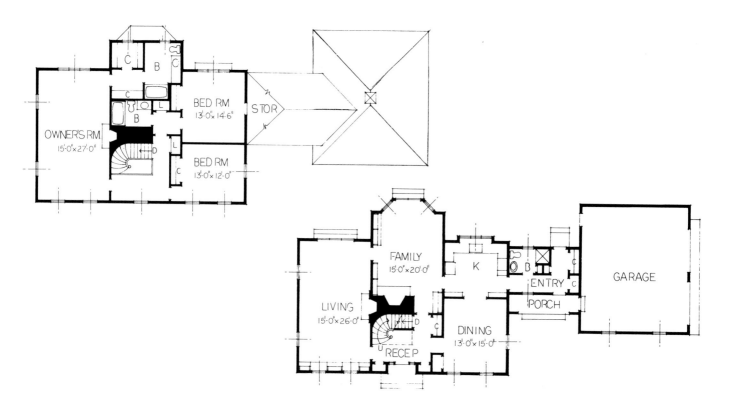

The graceful curve of this stair was created by an artist, but the man who produced it was both artist and craftsman.

Heat efficient they are not, but what is more welcome on a chilly night than an open fire?

A very difficult sloping site dictated that a retaining wall make the transition from drive to house.

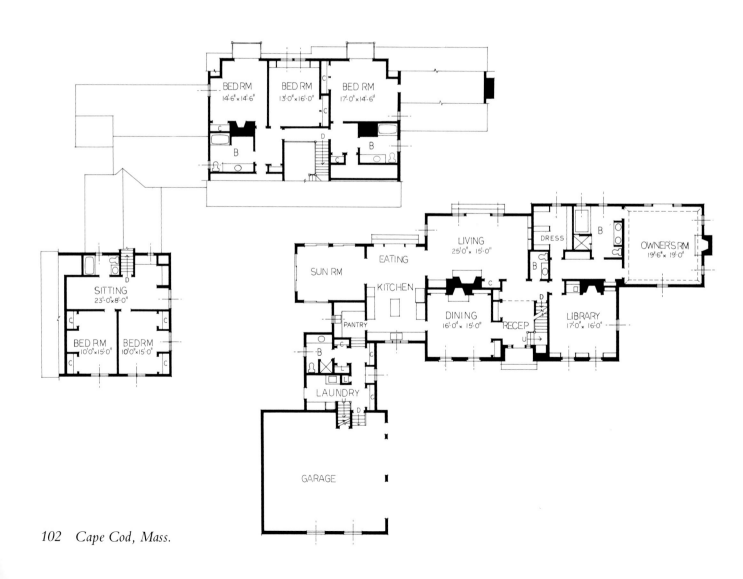

BED RM
14'-6" x 14'-6"

BED RM
13'-0" x 16'-0"

BED RM
17'-0" x 14'-6"

B

B

SITTING
23'-0" x 8'-0"

BED RM
10'-0" x 15'-0"

BEDRM
10'-0" x 15'-0"

SUN RM

EATING

KITCHEN

PANTRY

B

LAUNDRY

DINING
16'-0" x 15'-0"

LIVING
25'-0" x 15'-0"

DRESS

B

B

RECEP

LIBRARY
17'-0" x 16'-0"

OWNER'S RM
19'-6" x 19'-0"

GARAGE

The angled wings of this house provide protection from the cool sea breezes
and extends the use of terrace and pool in a climate where the outdoor
living season is short.

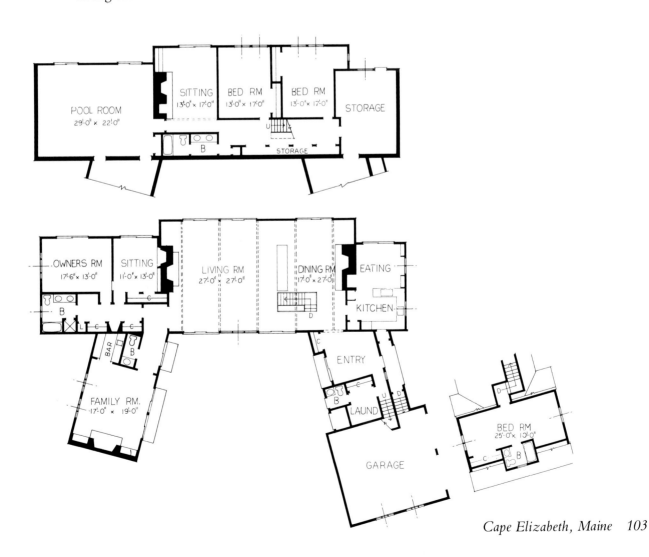

Low maintenance stained siding and no grass natural landscaping blend together on this wooded site. No ornamental detail except the round top window to feature the piano behind it.

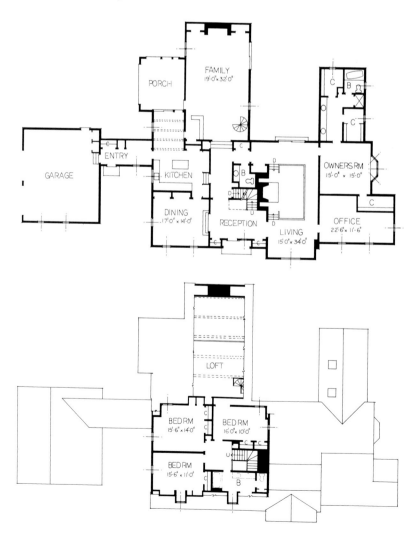

The double pitched hip roof is quite unusual and adds interest to the roof lines.

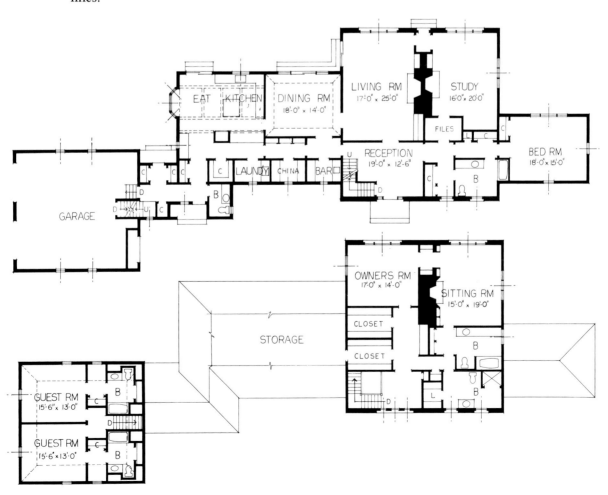

A large formal house can be overpowering if not skillfully designed. The wings, ells and angled appendages on this house kept it within the human scale.

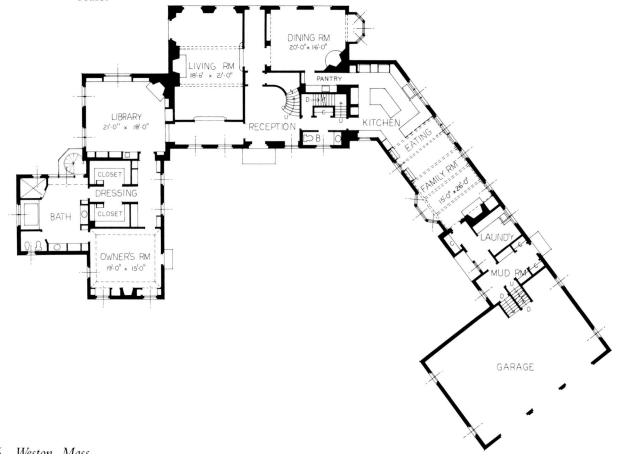

Simple detail is accented by brick quoins at the main corners and a four pilaster side lighted entrance.

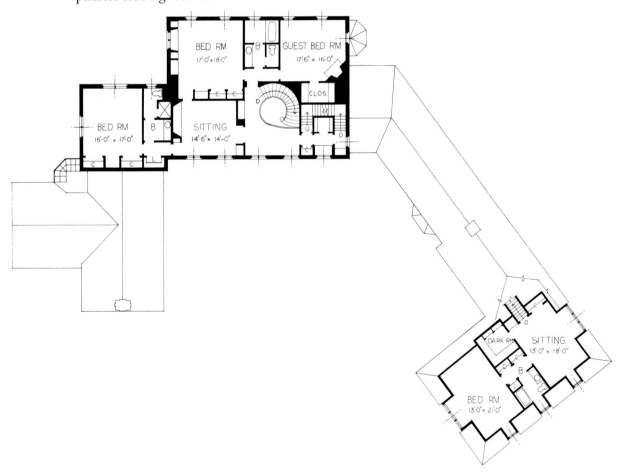

Simple detail is accented by brick quoins at the main corners and the four
pilaster side-lighted entrance.

Shoreland zoning restricted the building footprint to 30′ × 75′. The steeply pitched roofs, hipped dormers and varied fenestration are a pleasing combination.

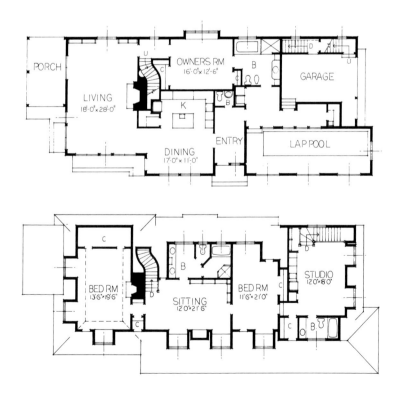

Painted narrow clapboards at the front and white cedar shingles left to weather naturally on the other walls is typical of the "Cape Cod" house.

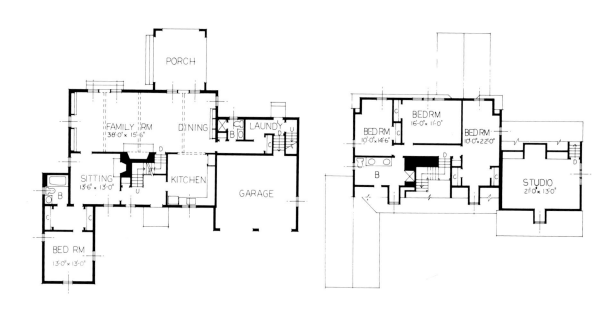

Stained clapboards, flush boards and cedar shake roof blend with the wooded site. One complements the other.

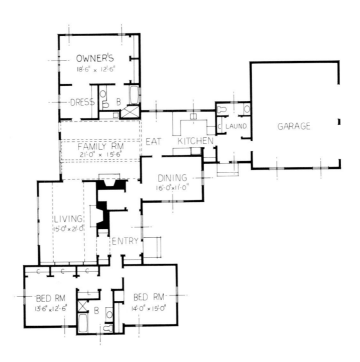

The "Half House" has practically all the elements of so called "Cape Cod" style. Large center chimney, narrow clapboards graduated near the grade, naturally weathered shingles and fenced in dooryard garden.

A close-up of the fence and dooryard garden.

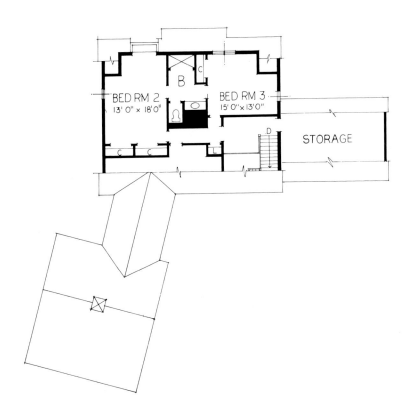

The "Tavern" bar area has a swing up grill (shown in the open position) when the Inn keeper is serving. This design is reminiscent of the bar at The Wayside Inn.

The Gathering Room has painted raised panel fireplace wall and the "Tavern" bar at the end of the room.

Another house designed for the community of New Seabury, on Cape Cod. Here again the basic masses of traditional Colonial architecture have been used. The plans and details are decidedly contemporary. The siding is large sheets of rough-sawn cedar plywood, stained brown and rubbed with white paint. Cedar-wood shakes cover the roof.

A large chimney, recalling those in the center of the houses of the early colonists, separates the kitchen and dining area from the living area. The steep ship's ladder provides access to the play-guest loft.

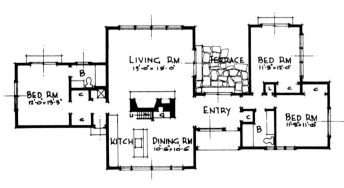

New Seabury, Mass.   115

The sandstone veneer, stained cedar siding and shake roof blend with natural surroundings of the site.

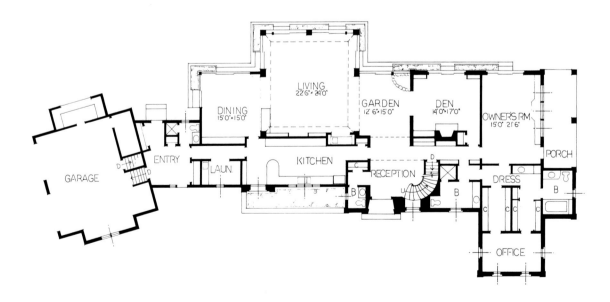

The same sandstone was used on the interior of the entrance hall. The detailing of the door and surround is oriental in feeling.

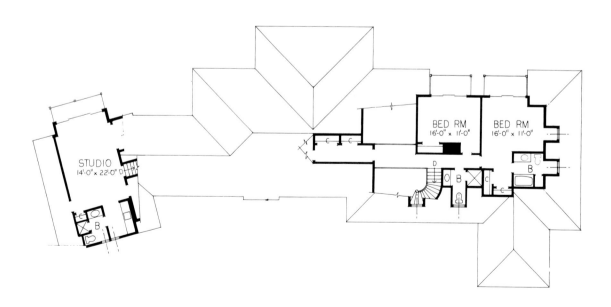

STUDIO
14'-0" x 22'-0" D

BED RM
16'-0" x 11'-0"

BED RM
16'-0" x 11'-0"

Built on a hillside that slopes to a salt water cove, this house commands a view almost to the White Mountains of New Hampshire. Natural colored materials were used for the exterior to blend with the pine and birch setting.

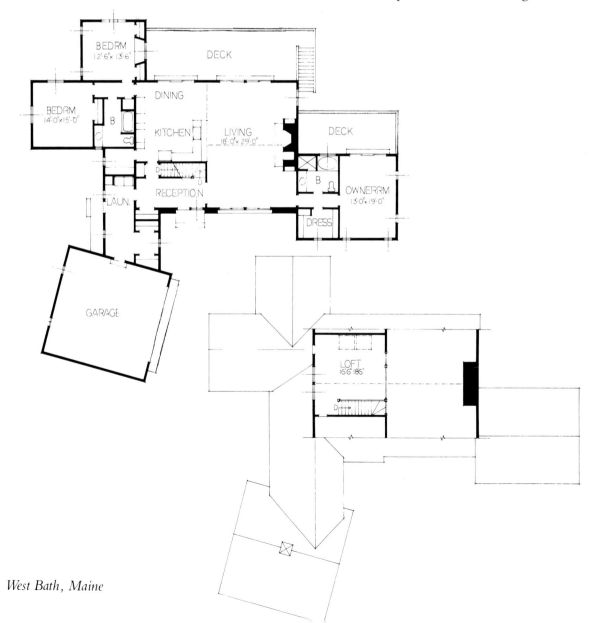

The field stone chimney and trussed ceiling dominate the living room. The wood storage is a hoist which can be dropped to the lower level, filled and then returned.

The recessed entrance is atypical of the "Cape Cod cottage" but very welcome in inclement weather.

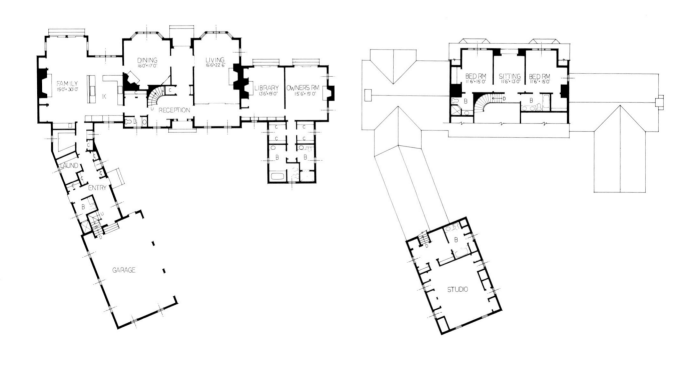

The off center entrance on the main façade is typical of an early Nantucket
house. However, the gambrel roof and whitewashed brick veneer are not.
An interesting variation.

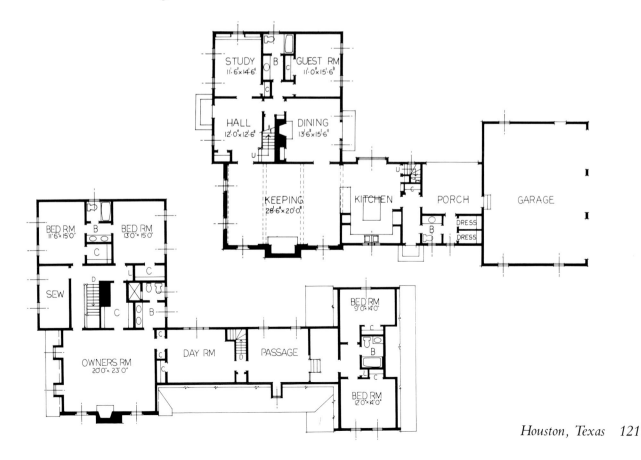

Twin bow windows flank a double door entrance. The use of different materials add interest and texture to a façade. The main house is whitewashed brick veneer with a service wing and garage sheathed with vertical boards.

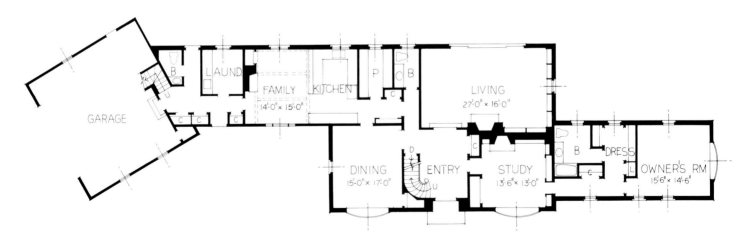

The house is sited in a field shielding the barn and paddock from the road.

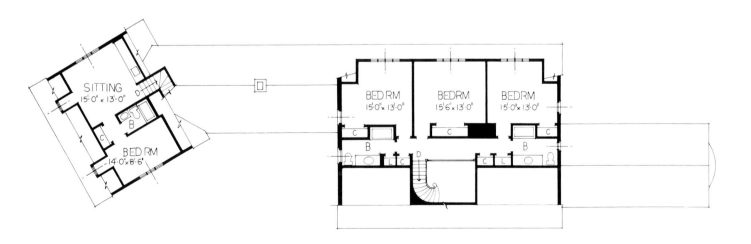

This could be a house but isn't. The Arthur Griffin Center for
Photographic Art is a gallery for photographic exhibits and a repository for
Arthur's thousands of images.

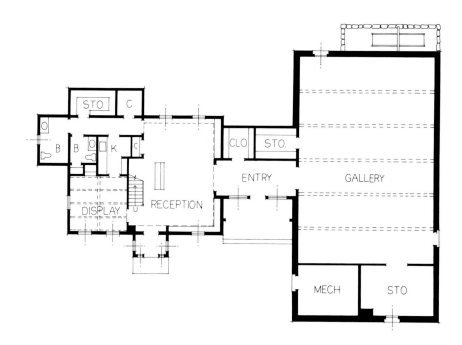

Reminiscent of an early New England grist mill, the stone building contains the Gallery and the "Miller's House", displays and administration.

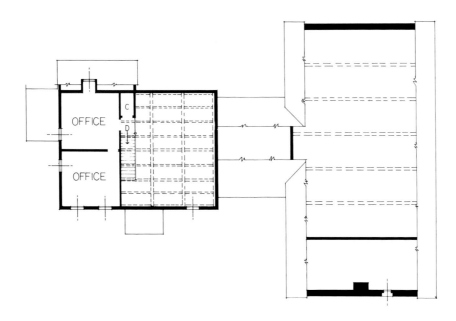

Eagle's Nest, a turn of the century summer cottage, was rebuilt and expanded for year 'round living.

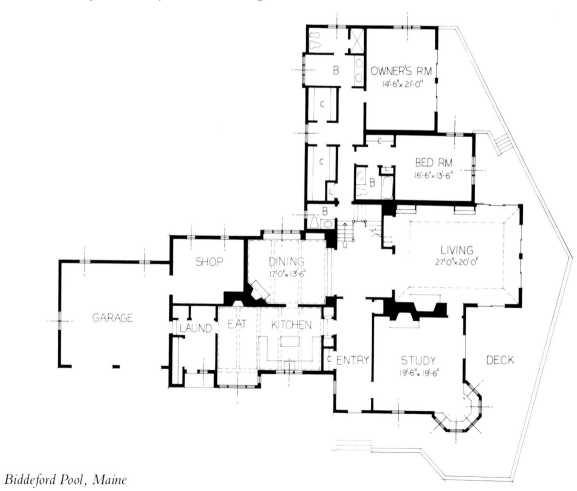

The southerly exposure provides passive solar gain in all rooms. The protected porch is a "sun pocket" on cool days.

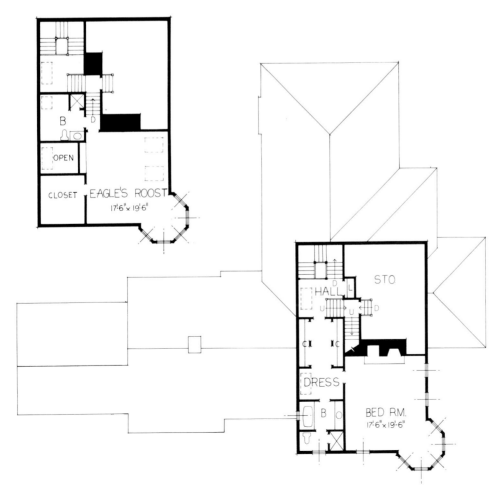

ENTRANCES
AND
OTHER DETAILS

(*Left*) An early eighteenth-century entrance. *Lunenberg, Mass.*

(*Below left*) Entrance of Royal Barry Wills' own house.

(*Below right*) Entrance of the Union Fork and Hoe Museum.

A simple entrance treatment for a Cape Cod Cottage, a transom over the door and flanking full height shutters.

The floor of this porch is paved with used sidewalk brick, the walls are wide pine sheathing, with a ceiling of hand trowelled plaster and old-hewn beams.

Entrance Detail

Main Entrance

Flush boards and quoins
play an important part in
this pedimented
doorway.

A paneled door with
pilasters and glass
transom over; wood "V"
gutter and brackets; all in
the best Cape Cod
tradition.

An inviting entrance adapted from the Georgian Period.

The arch detail on the chimney dormer, windows and entrance combine to bring the different elements together in the design.

The two story window is atypical of colonial design but here it focuses attention on the circular stair. (*Shown opposite.*)

A sweeping circular stair.

A gracefully curving stair with simple round balusters.

An early closed stringer stair.

Raised panels and three-piece cornice moulding frame the antique mantle and trumeau.

The paneled and pilastered fireplace breast has a slate facing. The narrowness of this facing contributes much to the delicacy and success of the design.

Antique paneling was used for the fireplace wall in the study below. The single pilaster is unique.

A modern cooking center with a barbecue. It shows that an efficient kitchen need not look sterile.

Royal Barry Wills Associates are noted primarily for domestic architecture but they also design public structures. The Christian Science Church in Winchester, Massachusetts, and the Centre Congregational Church in Lynnfield, Massachusetts, (*next page*) attest to their success in church architecture.

The chaste interior of the Lynnfield church is typical of the interior of
numerous old churches found all over New England.

A corporate headquarters